WORKBOOK

FOR

BREATHING UNDER WATER

SPIRITUALITY
AND THE
TWELVE STEPS

(A Practical Guide to Richard
Rohr's Book)

STELLA YAEL

THIS WORKBOOK BELONGS TO

HOW TO USE THIS WORKBOOK

Workbook for Breathing Under Water has been designed to improve your learning and assist you in understanding the major ideas and concepts covered in the original book more thoroughly. The goal of this section is to help you make the most of your journey toward personal development and introspection by advising you on how to use this workbook effectively.

1. Start with the Summary:
Reading the workbook's Summary section first will help you get a quick overview of the main points and takeaways from the original book. Before reading the remaining chapters, you should have a firm understanding of the book's main message thanks to this summary, which can also act as a reminder or introduction.

2. Explore the Chapters: Each chapter of this workbook focuses on a different subject or concept covered in the original book. Reading the chapter first will help you focus on the important ideas. Spend some time thinking about each lesson and how it relates to your own experiences and beliefs.

3. Practice Self-Reflection: Use the self-reflection prompts provided in each chapter after you've absorbed the key lessons. These inquiries are intended to promote serious contemplation and self-examination, promoting personal development and enabling you to use the information and insights from the original book to improve your own life. Spend some time considering the answers to these questions before filling out the spaces with your reflections. You'll learn

more about yourself, your beliefs, and your aspirations as a result of this self-reflection process.

4. Leverage the Self-Evaluation Questions: After you've read through all the chapters and done some introspection, focus on the section of the workbook's end that contains the Self-Evaluation Questions. These questions are intended to assist you in evaluating your development and the ways in which you've applied the book's lessons to your life. To gain insightful knowledge about your own personal development journey, answer these questions honestly and with thought.

5. Review and Revisit: As you work through this workbook, it's crucial to go back and go over your earlier responses and reflections. This will help you keep track of your development, spot trends, and spot any areas that may need more research or development. You can solidify your personal development by frequently reviewing your previous responses to help you remember the lessons you've learned.

Remember, this workbook is a tool for growth and self- discovery. Accept the process, be receptive to different viewpoints, and give yourself ample time to thoughtfully consider your own experiences. You can get the most out of this workbook and advance your personal development process by paying close attention to the key lessons and self-reflection questions and being open-minded about how you're doing.

The Workbook for Breathing Under Water will take you on a transformative journey, and I wish you luck and a rewarding experience.

With Love,
Stell Yael.

SUMMARY

Richard Rohr's "Breathing Under Water: Spirituality and the Twelve Steps" is a thought-provoking and insightful book. Rohr investigates the intersection of spirituality and addiction recovery using his experiences as a Franciscan priest and his understanding of twelve-step programs.

He begins by delving into the concept of addiction, arguing that it is not limited to overtly destructive behaviors such as substance abuse, but rather is a universal human struggle. He claims that everyone has addictive tendencies in their lives, whether it's through seeking approval, control, or unhealthy attachments. According to him, addiction is a coping mechanism for dealing with pain, emptiness, and a lack of connection, and everyone has their own unique way of numbing themselves.

The author then introduces the twelve-step program, emphasizing the spiritual nature of the process. He claims that the essence of these steps is surrendering to a higher power and admitting powerlessness over one's addictive behaviors. The author believes that the twelve steps provide a universal framework for spiritual transformation, offering a path to self-awareness, healing, and connection with a higher power.

The author then introduces the twelve-step program, emphasizing the spiritual nature of the process. He claims that the essence of these steps is surrendering to a higher power and admitting powerlessness over one's addictive behaviors. The author believes that the twelve steps provide a universal framework for spiritual transformation, offering a path to self-awareness, healing, and connection with a higher power.

In addition, he investigates the role of pain and suffering in the human experience. He contends that pain is a necessary catalyst for spiritual awakening and that true healing can only occur when one confronts and embraces their own woundedness. The author suggests that by acknowledging our brokenness, we can experience a profound sense of humility and an opening of the heart to both our own pain and the pain of others.

He also offers historical and biblical perspectives on the twelve steps, demonstrating their universality and timelessness. He draws parallels between Jesus' teachings and the principles of the twelve-step program, implying that both emphasize surrender, acceptance, forgiveness, and love.

In "Breathing Under Water," the author makes a compelling case for the integration of spirituality and addiction recovery. His profound insights, rooted in his own experiences and a deep understanding of both psychological and spiritual principles, provide readers with a new perspective on the nature of addiction as well as a path to spiritual transformation. Finally, the book serves as a guide for anyone seeking spiritual growth and healing, whether in the context of addiction recovery or the pursuit of a more fulfilling and meaningful life.

POWERLESSNESS

The author explores the concept of powerlessness as a necessary starting point on the path to spiritual growth and addiction recovery in this chapter.

He begins by stating that powerlessness is not a concept that our society typically embraces or even understands. We are instead taught to value self-sufficiency, independence, and control over our own lives. He contends, however, that true freedom and healing can come only when we recognize and accept our powerlessness.

The author then presents the first step of the twelve-step program, admitting that we have no control over our addiction and that our lives have become unmanageable. He explains that for addicts, this powerlessness is most obvious when they reach rock bottom and realize their addiction has taken control of their lives. However, he emphasizes that powerlessness is a universal condition that affects all humans, not just addicts.

He delves into the causes of this powerlessness, claiming that they are caused by our flawed and limited human nature. We are flawed by nature and prone to selfishness, ego, and a desire for control. He claims that our quest for power and control over our lives is futile because it contradicts the natural flow of life and spirituality.

The author then presents a different perspective on power: power that comes from surrendering and letting go. He introduces the concept of a higher power, which is central to twelve-step programs and spirituality in general. We can find true power and freedom by surrendering to this higher power, which is greater than ourselves and beyond our comprehension.

The author also looks at the role of suffering in realizing our powerlessness. He claims that suffering has the power to awaken us to our need for a higher power and to cause us to surrender our will. Suffering has the ability to shatter our egos and expose our powerlessness in ways that few other experiences can.

Finally, this chapter is a stimulating examination of the concept of powerlessness. According to the author, the first step toward true freedom and spiritual growth is to recognize and accept our powerlessness. He encourages readers to let go of their desire for control and surrender to a higher power, finding strength rather than weakness in powerlessness.

Key Points

1. Powerlessness is the first step toward spiritual and personal development. Recognizing our own limitations and admitting that we are not in control of everything allows us to be open to the possibility of healing and transformation.

2. Our powerlessness is the result of our addiction to control and obsession with achieving desired results. We become trapped in a cycle of attempting to control our circumstances, and we will never find true peace or freedom unless we surrender to a higher power.

3. Accepting our powerlessness allows us to grow in humility and surrender. We learn to trust in a higher power and seek guidance from a Higher Source rather than relying solely on our own willpower.

4. Lack of power does not imply weakness. It is not about being passive or resigned, but about accepting our limitations and being willing to relinquish control. It is a brave act that necessitates honesty and vulnerability.

5. We can discover a deep source of inner strength through powerlessness. By surrendering to a higher power, we gain access to a reservoir of wisdom, love, and grace that can help us navigate life's challenges.

We can experience healing, connection, and spiritual growth as a result of this transformative surrender.

EXERCISE ONE

1) Reflection and Visualization: Set aside some time each day to sit quietly and reflect on a time when you felt completely powerless. Close your eyes and try to imagine that moment as vividly as you can. Take note of any emotions or sensations that arise within you. Allow yourself to feel completely powerless. After a few moments, take a deep breath and slowly exhale, releasing any tension or resistance. Consider what this experience has taught you about yourself and your relationship with powerlessness.

2) Surrender and Letting Go: Pick an area of your life in which you resist or struggle with powerlessness. It could be a difficult relationship, a difficult work situation, or a personal habit you're trying to break. Practice surrendering to powerlessness every day by consciously letting go of control and expectations. When you notice yourself resisting or trying to control a situation, take a moment to pause and say a simple prayer or affirmation such as, "I let go of the need to control." In this situation, I accept my powerlessness." Allow yourself to believe in a higher power and let go of any attachments to results.

3) Compassionate Action: Find a way to assist others who are experiencing powerlessness in their own lives. This could be done by volunteering at a local shelter, joining a support group, or simply listening to someone in need. Acts of kindness and compassion should be directed toward those who are powerless. Pay attention to any judgments or assumptions that arise within you as you interact with others. Set aside your own power and privilege and try to truly empathize with their situations. Consider how acts of service and compassion can heal not only others, but also yourself, as you acknowledge the interconnectedness of all beings and the inherent power in humility and empathy.

Self Reflection Questions

How have you experienced powerlessness in your own life? What events or situations have made you feel powerless or out of control?

_____

_____

_____

_____

_____

How have you tried to regain a sense of power or control in unhealthy ways? What behaviors or patterns have you demonstrated when you were powerless?

_____

_____

_____

_____

How has spirituality aided you in overcoming feelings of powerlessness? Have you turned to a higher power or belief system for support and guidance during difficult times?

How can you learn to surrender and accept powerlessness as a natural part of life? What practices or strategies can you use to let go of the need for control and find peace in powerlessness?

_____

_____

_____

_____

_____

In what ways have you witnessed the destructive consequences of clinging to power and control? How has your fear of powerlessness affected your ability to fully engage in life and find fulfillment?

_____

_____

_____

_____

_____

_____

NOTES/REFLECTIONS

DESPERATE DESIRING

The author delves into the concept of desire and how it relates to addiction and spirituality in this chapter. He contends that addiction is a misdirected form of desire, and that true spiritual fulfillment can be found only by redirecting these desires toward a higher power.

The author begins by discussing the nature of addiction and how it is frequently fueled by feelings of dissatisfaction and longing. He explains that addicts seek the relief and fulfillment that they associate with the substance or behavior, rather than the substance or behavior itself. He claims that this intense desire is inherent in all humans and is a necessary part of our existence.

The problem, he claims, is that most people spend their lives attempting to satisfy these desires through external means such as material possessions, relationships, or achievements. He contends that this is a fruitless endeavor because these external sources of fulfillment are ultimately limited and transitory. Instead, the author contends that true fulfillment can be found only by turning inward and connecting with a spiritual source.

According to him, addiction is a desperate attempt to satisfy these deep desires, which are ultimately spiritual in nature. He describes addiction as a cycle of desire, satisfaction, and disappointment in which the addict constantly seeks to recreate the initial rush of fulfillment but is ultimately left feeling empty and unsatisfied. He claims that this is due to the addict's attempt to fill a spiritual void with a substance or behavior that can never truly provide lasting fulfillment.

The author uses the teachings of various spiritual traditions, including Christianity, Buddhism, and Hinduism, to make his point. He emphasizes detachment as a key principle in these traditions, emphasizing the need to let go of attachments to worldly desires in order to connect with a higher power. We can find true fulfillment and break the cycle of addiction by surrendering our individual will to a higher purpose.

He also discusses surrender as an important step in the recovery process. He explains that surrendering to a higher power necessitates admitting our powerlessness and admitting that our own efforts are inadequate.
He contends that this act of surrender opens the door to a spiritual transformation that can provide the fulfillment and healing that addicts crave.

The author emphasizes the link between addiction and the experience of pain in the chapter's final section.

He contends that addiction is frequently motivated by a desire to numb or escape from emotional or physical pain. He emphasizes facing and embracing our pain as a necessary step in our spiritual journey. Rather than avoiding or suppressing our pain, he encourages us to lean into it, to listen to and learn from it, and to find healing and transformation in the end.

Finally, the chapter delves into the concept of desire and its connection to addiction and spirituality. Addiction, according to the author, is a misguided attempt to satisfy deep desires that can only be satisfied through a spiritual connection. He believes that addicts can find true fulfillment and healing through surrender, detachment, and facing our pain. We can break the cycle of addiction and experience spiritual transformation by redirecting our desires toward a higher power.

Key Points

1. This chapter delves into the theme of addiction and how it relates to our most primal desires. It emphasizes that addiction is not limited to substance abuse and can take many forms, including workaholism, consumerism, and even excessive busyness.

2. The author contends that addiction stems from a fundamental dissatisfaction and longing within us, which he refers to as "desperate desiring" in this chapter.

He claims that our discontent stems from a disconnect with our true selves and a failure to recognize and embrace our inherent goodness.

3. According to the author, the addiction to our own will and the need to control our lives is the primary addiction that underpins all others. He contends that surrendering our will to a higher power, as advocated in the twelve-step program, is critical for spiritual growth and recovery.

4. The author examines the concept of powerlessness, which is a major theme in twelve-step recovery. He believes that embracing powerlessness does not imply weakness, but rather acknowledges the limitations of our human nature and our need for a higher power to guide us.

5. Finally, the author contends that changing our addictive patterns necessitates a spiritual awakening, a shift in consciousness that reconnects us with our true selves and allows us to surrender our desperate desire to a higher power. In order to find true freedom and fulfillment, we must be humble, surrender, and willing to let go of our self-will and control.

EXERCISE TWO

1. Spend some time reflecting on your own desperate desires. Write about one desire that frequently takes control of your life and prevents you from living in the present moment. Describe how this desire manifests in your thoughts, actions, and relationships. Investigate how this desire keeps you stuck and disconnected from your true self. Finally, imagine what it would be like to let go of this desperate desire and live a life of freedom and contentment. Write a brief reflection on the possibilities and challenges of releasing this desire.

2. Gather a group of people who have read this chapter. Begin the discussion by asking each person to share one desperate desire that they are struggling with. Encourage everyone to listen without judgment and to support one another. After everyone has shared, talk about the patterns and similarities in their desires, as well as how these desires affect their lives. Finally, brainstorm practical ways for the group to support one another in letting go of these desperate desires and moving toward healing and freedom.

3. Find a quiet and comfortable place where you can sit quietly for a few minutes. Close your eyes and take a few long breaths to center yourself. As you relax, imagine yourself standing on the edge of a peaceful lake.

Consider how the water reflects your mental calm. Now, visualize one desperate desire that you want to let go of. Consider this desire to be a heavy rock in your hands. Feel its weight and the energy it takes to hold on to it. Slowly imagine yourself tossing this rock into the lake and watching it sink beneath the surface. Feel a sense of relief and lightness in your body and mind as it fades. Take a few moments to enjoy your newfound freedom from your desperate desire. When you're ready, slowly open your eyes and take note of any insights or emotions that surfaced during this meditation.

Self Reflection Questions

In what ways do you frequently try to satisfy your deepest desires with superficial and temporary substitutes?

_____

_____

_____

_____

_____

How does your addiction to desire and desperation keep you from experiencing true surrender and reliance on a higher power?

_____

_____

_____

_____

_____

What role does your sense of entitlement and need for control play in your quest for fulfillment and peace?

_____

_____

_____

How can you learn to recognize and address the underlying wounds and traumas that fuel your desperate desires?

In what ways do you resist surrender and seek to avoid your pain and discomfort rather than face it head-on?

_____

_____

_____

_____

What practices and tools can you implement in your
life to gradually release your desperate desires and
find true contentment and serenity?

_____

_____

_____

_____

_____

_____

_____

NOTES/REFLECTIONS

SWEET SURRENDER

The author delves into the concept of surrender as a necessary step on the spiritual path to healing and wholeness in this chapter.

To begin, he emphasizes the importance of surrender in the twelve-step recovery process. He explains that surrender is not a sign of weakness or defeat, but rather of a willingness to relinquish control and hand over one's life to a Higher Power. Surrender necessitates a profound humility, an admission of our powerlessness in the face of addiction or destructive behaviors.

The author delves even deeper into the spiritual meaning of surrender. He contends that surrender is an active choice to align oneself with the divine will, rather than a passive act of resignation. Individuals who embrace surrender open themselves up to a transformative power that is greater than their own limited understanding and capacity.

According to him, surrender is a radical shift in consciousness because it allows people to step out of their ego-driven, self-centered mindset. He defines surrender as giving up the illusion of control and ego-driven desires in favor of trusting in a higher plan or purpose.

Surrender necessitates that people let go of their attachment to outcomes and embrace the present moment with acceptance and gratitude.

The author explains how surrender is frequently misunderstood and resisted because it contradicts our ego's need for control and security. Many people, he warns, prefer the illusion of control to the freedom and liberation that surrender can bring. Surrender requires people to face their fears and insecurities head on, trusting that a Higher Power will guide and support them through their trials.

He also emphasizes the role of suffering in surrender. He explains that when people surrender, they acknowledge and embrace their pain and suffering. He emphasizes, however, that surrender does not imply willingly accepting abuse or remaining in dangerous situations. Rather, surrender allows people to hold their suffering with compassion and courage, knowing that it can bring them value and growth.

The author concludes the chapter by explaining that surrender is a lifelong journey of letting go and opening oneself to divine guidance. He emphasizes the value of cultivating practices like prayer, meditation, and self-reflection in order to deepen one's surrender and nurture a relationship with the divine.

This chapter examines the transformative power of surrender on the spiritual path to healing and wholeness. The author emphasizes that surrender necessitates confronting one's ego, letting go of control, and trusting in a higher power. He emphasizes surrender's active choice and radical shift in consciousness, as well as the importance of embracing suffering with compassion. Finally, surrender is portrayed as a lifelong process that necessitates a dedication to spiritual practices as well as a willingness to continually let go and surrender to divine guidance.

Key Points

1. The importance of surrender in the spiritual journey and the twelve-step process is emphasized in this chapter. According to the author, surrender is not about giving up or losing, but rather about being willing to let go of our own will and trust in a higher power.

2. This chapter emphasized the paradoxical nature of surrender. The author explains that true freedom and transformation can only be found by surrendering our ego and control. He claims that surrender necessitates honesty, humility, and a willingness to work with grace.

3. The chapter delves into the concept of "sweet surrender," or willingly and joyfully surrendering. According to the author, true surrender is not forced,

but rather springs from a deep desire for healing and wholeness. He claims that surrendering to a higher power allows us to access a source of wisdom and guidance that is beyond our limited comprehension.

4. The author goes on to explain that surrender entails accepting and embracing our powerlessness. He contends that by admitting our limitations and relinquishing our need for control, we open ourselves up to the transformative power of grace. Surrender is the act of letting go and allowing something bigger to work within us.

5. The chapter concludes by emphasizing the transformative power of surrender, emphasizing that it is a continuous process throughout our spiritual journey rather than a one-time event. According to the author, surrender necessitates daily practice, prayer, and a willingness to surrender our will. He encourages readers to let go of their desires, attachments, and fears, understanding that true liberation and spiritual growth can only come from surrendering to a higher power.

EXERCISE THREE

1. Close your eyes and imagine fully surrendering to a situation or circumstance in your life that you have been clinging to. Allow yourself to experience the emotions that arise as a result of this process. Consider any insights or resistance that arise for you as you write down your reflections on what it would be like to truly let go and surrender.

2. Take out a pen and paper and begin by writing down the areas of your life where you find it difficult to surrender. It could be a habit, a relationship, a belief, or a fear. Next, consider why you find it difficult to let go of control in those areas. Are you worried about losing something? Do you have issues with trust? Write down freely and honestly about your emotions and experiences. Finally, think about some practical steps you can take to begin the surrendering process in those specific areas of your life. How can you integrate sweet surrender into your daily routine?

3. Look for a quiet, comfortable place to sit or lie down. Close your eyes and take a few long breaths to center yourself. Imagine yourself standing on the edge of a vast ocean as you continue to breathe deeply and calmly.
Feel the soft breeze against your skin and the warm sand beneath your feet.

Look out at the horizon and allow your eyes to be drawn to the seemingly endless expanse of water. Imagine that each wave crashing onto the shore represents a worry, fear, or burden that you are carrying. Choose to release that burden and surrender it to the ocean with each wave. Watch as it is swept away by the current and disappears into the depths. Continue this visualization for as long as you need, releasing one burden at a time. Reflect on how it feels to let go and surrender these burdens to a higher power as you finish. During this exercise, write down any insights or emotions that arise for you.

Self Reflection Questions

How have you experienced surrendering control in your life? What was the outcome of that experience?

In what areas of your life do you have the most difficulty letting go and surrendering to a higher power? Why do you think that is?

Reflecting on the concept of "sweet surrender," how can you apply it to your daily life and relationships?

_____

_____

_____

_____

_____

What beliefs or patterns of behavior might be preventing you from fully embracing the concept of surrender as discussed in the chapter?

_____

_____

_____

_____

_____

_____

How can you strengthen your faith in a higher power and develop a greater sense of surrender and acceptance?

_____

_____

_____

_____

_____

Can you think of any instances in your life where giving up control resulted in a positive outcome? How will you apply what you've learned in the future?

_____

_____

_____

_____

_____

_____

_____

What steps can you take to cultivate a more surrender-centered mindset during your recovery journey?

_____

_____

_____

_____

_____

_____

_____

NOTES/REFLECTIONS

A GOOD LAMP

In the context of the 12-step recovery process, this chapter delves into the essential qualities of a good spiritual guide or teacher.

The author begins by emphasizing the significance of a good lamp, a source of light that can guide us through our lives' darkness and confusion. The good lamp in the context of this book represents a spiritual guide who can assist us in navigating the path of recovery and spiritual growth.

A good spiritual guide, in his opinion, possesses several important characteristics. They must first have gone through their own healing journey, as they can only guide others where they have been. This indicates that the guide has confronted and overcome their own addictions or destructive patterns of behavior. This personal experience gives the guide credibility and allows them to empathize with those who seek their advice.

Second, a good spiritual guide acknowledges that they are not the final authority on truth or wisdom. They are humble enough to admit their limitations and point their seekers to something greater, whether that is God, a higher power, or a collective consciousness. They recognize that their role is simply to facilitate the seeker's spiritual journey, encouraging them to discover their own truth and connection to the divine.

Another important characteristic of a good guide, according to the author, is their ability to create a safe and non-judgmental environment. They do not impose their beliefs or values on their seekers, but rather provide an open and accepting environment for self-discovery and exploration. Individuals are free to express their doubts, fears, and struggles without fear of rejection or condemnation as a result of this. A good guide understands that each person's journey is unique and respects their process.

In addition, a good spiritual guide engages in active listening. They listen without interrupting or imposing their own agenda, and they are fully present to the seeker. This attentive listening allows the guide to gain a deeper understanding of the seeker, identify underlying patterns and issues, and provide guidance tailored to the individual's specific needs.

A good spiritual guide will also have a thorough understanding of the relationship between spirituality and the twelve-step recovery process. They are well-versed in the recovery principles and steps and can offer guidance and support within the framework of these tools. They recognize that recovery entails not only overcoming addiction but also cultivating a spiritual life that allows for long-term healing and growth.

In addition, he emphasizes the value of discernment in a spiritual guide. A good guide can tell the difference between what is beneficial and harmful to the spiritual journey of the seeker. They have wisdom and intuition, which allows them to guide people to practices, resources, and communities that will help them grow and heal.

In conclusion, this chapter looks at the characteristics of a good spiritual guide or teacher. Such a guide has been through their own healing journey, recognizes their own limitations, creates a safe and non-judgmental space, engages in active listening, understands the link between spirituality and recovery, and possesses discernment. The guide can effectively support individuals on their journey to spiritual growth and recovery by embodying these characteristics.

Key Points

1. The importance of self-awareness and self-knowledge as essential components of spiritual growth and recovery is emphasized in this chapter.

2. It emphasizes the importance of acknowledging our

own brokenness and embracing our shadow selves in order to experience true transformation.

3. The chapter suggests that we need a "good lamp" to illuminate the dark corners of our lives, referring to the spirituality and twelve-step program for guidance and wisdom.

4. The chapter delves into the idea that true spirituality is about fully embracing our humanity and discovering the divine within our own brokenness, rather than escaping or transcending it.

5. It emphasizes the importance of humility, surrender, and a willingness to let go of our own ego-driven desires and control in order to find spiritual wholeness and healing.

EXERCISE FOUR

1. Spend some time reflecting on your own shadow aspects, those aspects of yourself that you may have denied or repressed. Make a list of three characteristics or traits about yourself that you find difficult to accept. Examine why these aspects may be difficult for you and how accepting them may lead to growth and healing.

2. Find a quiet place and devote 10-15 minutes to guided meditation. Imagine holding a lamp that represents spiri-

tuality and the 12-step program. Allow the lamp's light to illuminate the dark corners of your life, bringing awareness and understanding to your own brokenness as you visualize it. Any insights or emotions that arise during this meditation should be noted.

3. Pick an area of your life where you tend to resist surrender or hold on to control. It could be a particular circumstance, relationship, or aspect of yourself. Reflect on why you find it difficult to let go and surrender in this area. Then, intentionally practice surrendering control in small ways. Begin by releasing control of one decision or outcome and observing how it feels. Examine any shifts or insights that emerge from this practice.

Self Reflection Questions

How well do you know yourself? Are you aware of your own strengths, weaknesses, and shadow aspects?

_____

_____

_____

Are you willing to acknowledge and embrace your
own brokenness? How does this awareness impact
your spiritual growth and recovery?

_____

_____

_____

_____

_____

Do you tend to seek spiritual growth as an escape
from your humanity, or are you willing to fully
embrace and integrate your brokenness into your
spiritual journey?

_____

How does humility play a role in your spiritual growth and recovery? Are you willing to surrender your ego-driven desires and control in order to find healing and wholeness?

What are some areas of your life where you may be resisting self-awareness and self-knowledge? How can you bring light to those dark corners and work towards transformation?

_____

_____

_____

_____

_____

How can you cultivate a deeper sense of surrender and willingness in your spiritual journey? What steps can you take to let go of control and open yourself up to healing? bit

_____

_____

_____

_____

NOTES/REFLECTIONS

ACCOUNTABILITY/ SUSTAINABILITY

In relation to the twelve steps of recovery, this chapter focuses on the concepts of accountability and sustainability. The author delves into the significance of these principles in achieving spiritual growth and transformation.

The chapter begins by emphasizing the importance of accountability, which entails accepting personal responsibility for our actions, behaviors, and the consequences they cause. According to the author, accountability is a critical step in the recovery process because it forces us to confront the reality of our destructive patterns and take responsibility for our lives. He emphasizes that only through accountability will we be able to break free from the vicious cycle of self-deception and denial, and eventually embark on the path to healing and recovery.

He also emphasizes the importance of embracing sustainability in our spiritual journey, explaining that recovery is a continuous process that requires ongoing engagement and commitment. In this context, sustainability refers to the long-term practices, disciplines, and habits required to live a healthy and balanced lifestyle. These include engaging in spiritual practices on a regular basis, cultivating a support network, and being mindful of our thoughts, actions, and relationships. He contends that without sustainability, our recovery growth and progress are likely to be fleeting, as we are prone to reverting to old patterns and destructive behaviors.

To demonstrate the principles of accountability and sustainability, the author draws on the wisdom of the twelve steps, which are a cornerstone of recovery programs. He emphasizes the importance of step four, which involves conducting a fearless and in-depth moral inventory of ourselves, as a critical step toward accountability. We can begin the healing process by reflecting on our past behaviors and acknowledging the harm we have caused.

The author provides practical advice on how to cultivate sustainability in our lives, recommending practices such as meditation, regular self-reflection, and participation in a supportive community. He emphasizes the importance of developing a spiritual discipline that aligns with our values and allows us to connect deeply with our inner selves and a higher power. We can nurture our spiritual growth and maintain our recovery by incorporating these sustainable practices into our daily lives.

Furthermore, the author investigates the relationship between accountability and sustainability. He contends that accountability is the foundation for long-term sustainability. Our efforts to achieve sustainable growth are likely to fail unless we accept responsibility for our actions and embrace accountability. Similarly, without long-term practices, an emphasis on accountability may become overwhelming and unsustainable.

Finally, in the context of recovery, this chapter delves into the critical concepts of accountability and sustainability. The importance of these principles in enabling individuals to break free from destructive patterns, cultivate spiritual growth, and maintain long-term recovery is emphasized by the author. We take ownership of our actions and have the opportunity to make amends when we embrace accountability, while sustainability ensures that we engage in sustainable practices and disciplines that support our ongoing growth and healing. This chapter provides insightful and practical advice for individuals seeking to incorporate these principles into their recovery journey and spiritual transformation.

Key Points

1. Accountability is an important part of the spiritual journey and is closely related to sustainability. It is difficult to remain committed to the transformative jour-

ney and is closely related to sustainability. It is difficult to remain committed to the transformative process of the twelve steps without accountability.

2. Accountability entails being truthful and open with oneself and others about one's flaws, failures, and shortcomings. It necessitates a willingness to look at one's own flaws and accept responsibility for one's actions.

3. Accountability is fostered in the context of the twelve steps through regular meetings with a sponsor or spiritual guide who can provide guidance, support, and help hold the individual accountable to their recovery goals.

4. The concept of sustainability entails not only achieving temporary change, but also maintaining that change over time. To avoid relapse and continue spiritual growth, sustained recovery necessitates ongoing effort, commitment, and accountability.

5. Accountability and sustainability are inextricably linked to humility. To hold oneself accountable and maintain one's recovery, one must cultivate humility and recognize one's own limitations while remaining open and willing to learn from others.

EXERCISE FIVE

1. Reflect on your daily actions and choices, and write a journal entry about how you can improve your personal accountability in your relationships, work, and community. Consider the impact of your decisions on others and how you can align your actions with the principles of compassion, honesty, and integrity. Identify specific areas where you can improve and outline practical steps you can take to improve your accountability.

2. Conduct an honest assessment of your environmental footprint and level of sustainability. Examine your consumption habits, waste generation, and energy usage. Consider the potential effects of these habits on the planet and future generations. Identify at least three concrete changes you can make to reduce your environmental impact, such as investing in renewable energy sources, reducing single-use plastic, or supporting local, sustainable businesses. Track and evaluate your progress over the next month.

3. Join or form a small accountability group with friends who are also interested in personal growth and sustainability. Schedule regular meetings to discuss and evaluate your progress in both areas. Share your successes and challenges, offer support, and hold each

other accountable for the actions you agreed to take. Use this supportive space to learn from one another, share resources and ideas, and inspire one another's personal and collective transformation.

Self Reflection Questions

Do you accept responsibility for your actions and the consequences, or do you blame others or external factors?

Are you clear on the values and principles that guide your actions and decisions?

How do you develop personal accountability without succumbing to self-punishment or guilt?

Are you open to receiving feedback and criticism from others, and do you use it to help you grow and improve?

_____

_____

_____

_____

_____

_____

How are you actively participating in your own spiritual and emotional healing and transformation?

_____

_____

_____

_____

_____

NOTES/REFLECTIONS

THE CHICKEN OR THE EGG: WHICH COMES FIRST?

The author delves into the concept of causality and the interaction of human action and divine intervention in the process of spiritual transformation in this chapter.

The author begins by discussing the contradictory nature of spirituality. According to him, the spiritual journey is non-linear and frequently involves a duality of cause and effect.

In order to illustrate the relationship between human effort and God's grace in the process of spiritual growth, he uses the question "Which comes first, the chicken or the egg?"

The author emphasizes the importance of surrendering one's ego and admitting powerlessness over addiction or destructive behaviors, drawing on the Twelve Steps program's teachings. He considers surrender to be the first step toward spiritual transformation. Recognizing the limits of our own power and control allows God's grace to work in our lives.

The ego-driven paradigm, according to the author, perpetuates the illusion of self-sufficiency and prevents people from experiencing true freedom. He contends that true spiritual development necessitates the death of the ego. We can only be open to the transformative power of God's grace if we let go of our attachment to ego-centered desires.

While recognizing the importance of personal responsibility and accountability, the author emphasizes that the transformational process is ultimately rooted in God's initiative. He notices that many people in recovery are powerless and broken before seeking help from a higher power. This act of surrender is not a passive resignation, but rather an active decision to align oneself with divine guidance.

The author also discusses grace as God's undeserved favor. He explains that grace is a gift freely given by God, not something that can be earned or obtained through human effort. He cautions against using this interpretation of grace to justify inaction or irresponsibility. Rather, he encourages readers to take an active role in their own recovery and personal growth while also acknowledging their reliance on divine intervention.

The author delves into the theme of paradox in spirituality and recovery in the latter part of the chapter. He claims that the spiritual journey is riddled with paradoxes and contradictions, such as the idea that surrendering control leads to true freedom or that accepting powerlessness opens the door to strength. He claims that these paradoxes are meant to provide opportunities for spiritual growth and transformation rather than to be solved or resolved.

Finally, the author stresses the importance of community and fellowship in the healing process. Individuals, he believes, cannot embark on a spiritual journey alone; rather, they require the support and guidance of others who have traveled similar paths. He emphasizes the importance of vulnerability and authenticity in these relationships, as true healing and transformation can take place only in an atmosphere of trust and acceptance.

In summary, in the process of spiritual transformation, this chapter delves into the complex relationship between human action and divine intervention. The author delves into spirituality's contradictory nature, emphasizing the importance of surrender, grace, and personal responsibility. He also talks about the importance of community and fellowship in the recovery process. Overall, this chapter provides valuable insight into the interconnectedness of human effort and God's grace, as well as useful guidance for those seeking spiritual growth and recovery.

Key Points

1. Our understanding of spirituality and the twelve steps can benefit from the application of the chicken or the egg dilemma. The author contends that because the spiritual and practical facets of recovery are intertwined, we cannot truly separate them.

2. According to the author, conventional twelve-step programs have mainly concentrated on the pragmatic aspects of recovery, like abstinence and behavioral modification. But he holds that both the material and spiritual facets must be integrated for true transformation to occur.

3. The author emphasizes how the twelve steps had their origins in a spiritual approach to recovery that heavily drew from Christianity. But as time went on, the emphasis shifted to a more secular viewpoint, causing a division between spirituality and recovery.

4. The author stresses the value of reclaiming the twelve steps' spiritual foundations because they offer a deeper and more comprehensive understanding of recovery. He contends that addressing the spiritual components can result in a more significant and long-lasting transformation.

5. By acknowledging that spirituality comes first, the debate over whether the chicken or the egg came first is finally resolved. People can access a source of power and direction that aids them in their recovery journey by acknowledging and yielding to a higher power.

EXERCISE SIX

1. Think about a time in your life when you faced the "Chicken or the Egg" dilemma. Create a journal entry in which you investigate the root cause of the situation and whether your actions influenced the outcome or the situation itself. Consider how this reflection can help you improve your self-awareness and personal growth.

2. Lead a group discussion on the topic of cause and effect in addiction and recovery. Encourage participants to share their personal experiences and insights into whether addiction behaviors are the result of pre-existing conditions or if the addiction itself causes further destructive behaviors. Try to find common ground as a group and discover ways to break this cycle by focusing on the underlying spiritual principles discussed in the book.

3. Hold a "Chicken or the Egg" thought experiment to encourage participants to critically analyze societal issues such as poverty, inequality, or addiction.

Encourage them to consider whether these issues are the result of individual choices or if they are systemic issues that perpetuate destructive cycles. Engage in an open dialogue in which participants can challenge assumptions and consider alternative viewpoints.

Self Reflection Questions

Does your addiction result from a deep-seated spiritual emptiness or from experiences and circumstances outside of your control?

_____

_____

_____

_____

_____

_____

How has your addiction affected your capacity to engage in spiritual practice and connect with others?

_____

_____

_____

_____

_____

_____

_____

Do you use your addiction to try to fill a void inside of yourself or as a means of escape from the suffering and discomfort of life?

_____

_____

_____

_____

_____

_____

_____

Have you ever thought that your lack of spiritual fulfillment or a connection to a higher power could be the cause of your addiction?

_____

_____

_____

_____

_____

_____

How can you start to develop a more profound spirituality in order to deal with the root causes of your addiction?

_____

_____

_____

_____

_____

How has your addiction impeded your spiritual development and kept you from fully knowing peace and tranquility?

_____

_____

_____

_____

_____

_____

In order to achieve long-term recovery and personal transformation, are you prepared to confront and address the spiritual causes of your addiction?

_____

_____

_____

_____

_____

NOTES/REFLECTIONS

WHY DO WE NEED TO ASK

The author examines the value of seeking assistance and the effectiveness of surrender in the process of spiritual development and healing in this chapter.

He starts off by emphasizing the widespread social stigma associated with asking for assistance. He contends that this resistance stems from our aversion to being exposed and our need to keep control of our lives. He contends, however, that real development and transformation can only occur when we are willing to admit our shortcomings and accept help.

The idea of surrender and its significance in the process of recovery are then explored by the author. He explains that giving up is an act of courage and strength rather than weakness. By giving up control, we admit that we are powerless over every aspect of our lives and that we require a higher power or a support system.

The author makes clear that seeking assistance and giving up go hand in hand. He claims that we make room for the divine to act in our lives by letting go of our self-will and ego. We allow ourselves to be open to the possibility of receiving direction and assistance from a higher power through this surrender.

The author also examines how asking for assistance involves the community. He emphasizes the value of finding a caring environment where people can open up about their challenges and get the support they require. For those looking for recovery and growth, this community—whether it be a twelve-step program or a spiritual organization—serves as a source of support and direction.

He emphasizes that while asking for assistance necessitates a certain amount of humility and vulnerability, it is only through this process that we can truly experience liberation and discover our true selves. According to him, the road to recovery is essentially a journey to let go of our false selves and accept who we really are.

This chapter's conclusion discusses the importance of seeking assistance and giving up in the course of spiritual development and recovery. The author draws attention to the resistance we frequently experience when seeking assistance and stresses the significance of letting go of self-will and ego in order to be open to divine guidance and assistance. He also stresses the significance of finding a caring environment where people can open up about their challenges and get the sympathy and support they require. In the end, the chapter emphasizes the liberating potential of vulnerability, humility, and surrender on the path to real liberation and self-discovery.

Key Points

1. The key to spiritual development is acknowledging our helplessness and seeking assistance. Our society frequently encourages independence, self-reliance, and the appearance of control, but real change can only take place when we humbly admit our shortcomings and ask for help from a higher power.

2. Asking necessitates letting go of our ego's need for control and embracing a position of vulnerability. This act of surrender is not a sign of helplessness but rather a brave move in the direction of strengthening our relationship with the divine. Our lives become more accessible for God's grace to enter and lead us toward healing and transformation when we let go of our ego and ask for assistance.

3. Being open and honest about our needs and limitations is crucial, as this chapter emphasizes. It promotes a sense of belonging and interconnectedness to be willing to ask for what we need. By being open and vulnerable with others, we not only open the door for understanding and support, but we also foster a climate in which others feel safe and encouraged to seek assistance themselves.

4. Another topic covered in this chapter is the function of prayer as a means of requesting. The practice of surrender and receptivity that is prayer goes beyond asking for things or looking for answers. We give a higher power access to us through prayer so that they can provide us with direction, wisdom, and grace. Our faith in God is bolstered and our spiritual connection is strengthened when we develop a daily prayer practice.

5. The final topic covered in the chapter deals with the resistance and fear that frequently surface when we consider asking for assistance. In order to understand these fears as ego-based illusions, readers are urged to face them head-on. It takes courage and humility to ask for help; it is not a sign of weakness. A true healing and growth can only take place when we let go of our ego's need for control and embrace the vulnerability of asking. In doing so, we expose ourselves to the grace's transformative power.

EXERCISE SEVEN

1. Take some time to journal about a recent situation in which you were hesitant to seek assistance or clarification. What were the reasons for your reluctance to ask? What effect did it have on the outcome or your well-being? What would have happened if you had asked for help?

2. Gather a small group of friends or coworkers and talk about asking for help. Share personal experiences in which asking for help made a positive difference or in which not asking for help caused problems. Consider any patterns or fears that arise from your stories. Discuss what collective strategies or mindsets you can develop to overcome these obstacles and create a culture of asking for help within your group or community.

3. Find a quiet and comfortable place to relax. Close your eyes and imagine yourself in a situation where you confidently ask for assistance and receive all the help and support you need. Picture the positive outcomes of your willingness to ask. Notice how it feels to release any resistance or fear. Take a few minutes to soak in this visualization, and then slowly come back to the present moment.

Self Reflection Questions

How frequently do you avoid difficult questions or uncomfortable truths in your life?

_____

_____

_____

_____

_____

_____

_____

_____

Do you have any behavioral patterns that indicate a fear of facing the truth or asking difficult questions?

_____

_____

_____

_____

_____

_____

How can you incorporate the practice of self-inquiry and asking deeper questions into your daily life?

_____

_____

_____

_____

_____

_____

How does your spirituality align with the concept of admitting powerlessness and surrendering control?

_____

_____

_____

_____

_____

_____

Do you have any personal beliefs or assumptions that you need to challenge in order to advance your spiritual growth and understanding?

_____

_____

_____

_____

_____

Have you avoided asking for help or support from others when faced with difficulties in your life? How can you break this cycle?

_____

_____

_____

_____

_____

NOTES/REFLECTIONS

PAY BACK TIME

The author delves into the concept of making amends and seeking forgiveness in this chapter.

The author begins by emphasizing that seeking forgiveness is about healing ourselves as well as repairing relationships with others. He contends that the inability to forgive oneself is a major cause of addiction, as people frequently turn to destructive behaviors to numb their guilt and shame.

The author emphasizes that making amends is more than just apologizing; it also entails accepting responsibility for one's actions and actively working to repair the harm done to others. He explains that making amends is an uncomfortable and humble process, but it is a necessary step toward spiritual growth and long-term sobriety.

When making amends, he emphasizes the importance of sincerity and genuineness. He advises people to be open to hearing the other person's point of view without becoming defensive or justifying their actions. According to him, the act of truly listening fosters empathy and allows the individual to experience the consequences of their previous actions.

According to the author, making amends should be a continuous process rather than a one-time event. He emphasizes the importance of consistency and follow-through in order to rebuild trust and relationships. He also admits that not all amends will be accepted or returned, and that disappointment or rejection may occur. He does, however, suggest that the most important thing is to make amends from a genuine place and to let go of any expectations for a specific outcome.

The author also touches on the idea of making amends to oneself. He contends that self-forgiveness is essential for personal growth and healing. He encourages people to be compassionate to themselves and to let go of self-judgment and self-condemnation.

Furthermore, the author acknowledges that making amends can be a delicate process, particularly when the harm done is severe or making amends could potentially cause additional harm. To navigate these situations with wisdom and discernment, he recommends seeking advice from a trusted mentor, sponsor, or therapist.

Overall, this chapter makes a compelling case for making amends and seeking forgiveness as necessary steps toward recovery and spiritual transformation. The author offers practical advice and insights into how to approach the process of making amends with sincerity, humility, and an open heart. He emphasizes that through these actions, people can begin to heal their own wounds and mend broken relationships, paving the way for a new and healthier way of life.

Key Points

1. In the context of spirituality and the twelve steps, the concept of "pay back time" refers to the idea that individuals who have experienced a transformative spiritual awakening are motivated to live a life of service and gratitude, giving back to others what they have received.

2. Returning the gift of grace and compassion can take many forms, including sharing one's personal experience, strength, and hope with those in need, offering support and encouragement to those in need, and actively participating in service work and acts of kindness.

3. Participating in pay back time is not only a way to express gratitude for one's own spiritual transformation, but it is also a way to deepen one's spiritual growth and relationship with a higher force or divine presence.

4. Paying it forward is not about obligation or duty; it is a response to the individual's overwhelming love and grace. It is an expression of the realization that the gift of

transformation cannot be kept to oneself but must be shared with others.

5. Paying it forward is a way of being and living in the world that is not limited to specific actions or activities. It entails a continuous commitment to selfless acts of love, compassion, and service, both large and small, in daily life.

EXERCISE EIGHT

1. Take some time to think about times in your life when you felt a strong desire for vengeance or payback. Write down these incidents and reflect on the emotions you felt at the time. What were the underlying motivations for your desire for vengeance? How did it make you feel? Did it give you any satisfaction or relief? Reflect on any lessons you learned from these experiences and how they shaped your understanding of the concept of payback.

2. Choose someone in your life who you believe has wronged you or harmed you. It could be someone from your past or someone you currently interact with. Write a letter to this person expressing your genuine feelings and emotions about what they did. After you've written the letter, read it carefully and consider whether holding onto your resentment and desire for vengeance is serving

you in any way. Reflect on the potential benefits of forgiveness and the freedom it could bring you. Take a few moments to meditate or pray, focusing on letting go of your desire for vengeance and holding a space of compassion and forgiveness in your heart for the person identified.

3. Make a list of five people who have had a positive impact on your life or helped you in some way. Think about each person and the impact they have had on you. Write a brief thank-you note to each person, expressing your appreciation for their presence in your life and the ways in which they have supported or inspired you. Think about how these people have shown you kindness, love, or compassion without expecting anything in return. Consider the concept of payback and how it contrasts with the actions of those for whom you are grateful. Take some time to meditate or pray, expressing gratitude to a higher power for the blessings of these people in your life and offering a willingness to let go of any desire for retaliation in favor of a more peaceful and loving approach.

Self Reflection Questions

How has the idea of "paying back time" struck a chord in your own life?

_____

_____

_____

_____

_____

How have you retaliated against people who have wronged you or tried to "get even" with them?

_____

_____

_____

_____

_____

_____

_____

How have your retaliation attempts ultimately hurt you and other people?

_____

_____

_____

_____

_____

_____

Have you ever had genuine reconciliation and forgiveness? If so, what happened and how did it affect you personally?

_____

_____

_____

_____

_____

_____

_____

Do you regularly find yourself blaming others for your errors or have you truly accepted responsibility for your own actions and behaviors?

_____

_____

_____

_____

_____

_____

_____

How can you start to change your outlook from one of seeking recompense to one of seeking recovery and development?

_____

_____

_____

_____

_____

How can you demonstrate forgiveness and show grace to other even when it may be challenging or uncomfortable?

_____

_____

_____

_____

_____

NOTES/REFLECTIONS

SKILLFUL MEANS

In this chapter, the author examines the idea of "skillful means" and how it relates to the practice of the twelve steps and one's spiritual journey.

The author starts by defining "skillful means" as a Buddhist concept that refers to using the proper techniques or tactics to assist others in experiencing spiritual growth. The twelve steps, according to him, can be thought of as a type of effective means that people can use to get over their addictions and reestablish their connection to a higher power. He stresses the need for both grace and effort in spiritual growth, and the twelve steps offer a framework that combines both.

The discussion of meditation as a spiritual practice and effective tool follows. He emphasizes the value of meditation for calming the mind, improving self-awareness, and encouraging a closer relationship with God or a higher power. He emphasizes that practicing meditation is more about developing a practice of surrender and allowing oneself to be transformed from within rather than about achieving a particular result or attaining a state of perfection.

Additionally, the author adds that using skillful means entails accepting pain and suffering as chances for development and transformation. According to him, addiction is frequently an effort to dull or escape from pain, but genuine healing can only take place when a person is prepared to confront and deal with their pain. Instead of attempting to avoid or mask their pain with addictive behaviors, people who use the twelve steps can face their pain head-on and find the strength to move through it.

The value of community in the process of spiritual development is another topic he covers. To truly comprehend and navigate the difficulties of addiction and recovery, he explains that we need the support and direction of others who have traveled a similar path. With skillful means, community offers the setting for exchanging and learning from one another's experiences as well as the accountability to adhere to the twelve steps.

The concept of "the practice of presence" is explored by the author as a different type of skillful means toward the end of the chapter. Instead of getting caught up in the past or worrying about the future, he emphasizes the value of being fully present and involved in each moment. People can develop a stronger connection with themselves, others, and a higher power by practicing presence, which results in a feeling of fulfillment and peace.

This chapter concludes by delving into the idea of skillful means and examining how it relates to following the Twelve Steps and the spiritual path. In order to overcome addiction and reestablish a connection with a higher power, the author emphasizes the significance of effective methods. In his discussion of the spiritual development process, he touches on topics such as meditation, accepting pain and suffering, community, and practicing presence. He offers advice and insight on how to deal with the difficulties of addiction and achieve healing and transformation through this exploration.

Key Points

1. Skillful means refers to the various tactics and methods that can be used to guide people through their spiritual journey and healing process. It emphasizes the significance of meeting people where they are and adapting the strategy to suit their particular needs and circumstances.

2. The chapter emphasizes the significance of a holistic approach to spirituality and recovery, which takes into account a person's physical, emotional, mental, and spir-

itual needs. It emphasizes how these dimensions are interconnected and how each one must be addressed in order to experience genuine healing and growth.

3. Recognizing that no one spiritual practice or tradition is right for everyone, skillful means encourages people to be open to various spiritual practices and traditions. It promotes an openness to investigating various ideologies while honoring and gaining knowledge from the wisdom of various traditions.

4. The chapter places a strong emphasis on the role that community and support play in the healing process. It emphasizes how crucial it is to locate and get involved with a supportive group that has similar beliefs and objectives because doing so offers people a nurturing and secure environment in which to further their spirituality and recovery.

5. Capable methods also emphasizes the value of consistent spiritual practices like prayer, meditation, and introspection. These techniques support people in developing a stronger bond with their Higher Power or a transcendent reality, which offers support, fortitude, and peace as they face the difficulties of recovery. The development of self-awareness, mindfulness, and a sense of purpose—all of which are necessary for maintaining long-term recovery—are also aided by these practices.

EXERCISE NINE

1. Reflect on a recent event or interaction in your life where you had the opportunity to use tact. Consider how you might have reacted differently to produce a more favorable outcome as you write down your thoughts.

2. Think of a heated discussion or argument you have been avoiding or dreading. Consider how using the idea of skillful means might enable you to approach this discussion with insight and compassion. Make a plan in your journal for how you'll apply skillful means to your strategy, taking into account things like active listening, empathy, and nonjudgmental communication.

3. Look for a place that is peaceful and quiet where you can unwind for a while. Breathe deeply for a few breaths, slowly and deliberately inhaling and exhaling. Concentrate on developing a sense of mindfulness and awareness in the present moment as you continue to breathe.

Think back to a recent interaction or situation where you could have used tactful means once you've regained your composure and sense of grounding. Allow yourself to remember the specifics of the circumstance, but make an effort to observe them objectively and detachedly. Simply take note of your reaction or response at the time.

Currently, visualize yourself mentally reliving that circumstance. Imagine using effective means to respond this time. Imagine that you are responding with insight, understanding, and compassion. How would your language and behavior change? What changes would be made to the outcome?

Spend a few minutes reflecting on this new perspective and recognizing the opportunity for interactional development and transformation. Open your eyes when you're ready and write in your journal about the lessons you've learned from this exercise. Think about how you can use the principles of skillful means in your interactions going forward.

Self Reflection Questions

What is your current perspective on "skillful means" in your life? Do you believe in the power of intentional action and how it can help you on your spiritual growth journey?

_____

_____

_____

_____

_____

How have you successfully navigated challenges or difficult situations in the past? How did this approach affect your overall well-being and interpersonal relationships?

_____

_____

_____

_____

_____

_____

Considering your own relationship with spirituality and the twelve steps, how open are you to incorporating skillful means into your daily practices? Is there any resistance or hesitancy, and if so, how can you overcome it?

_____

_____

_____

_____

_____

_____

What qualities or characteristics do you believe are required to effectively use skillful means? How can you develop or cultivate these qualities in yourself?

_____

_____

_____

Reflecting on your current spiritual practices, what changes can you make to ensure that skillful means become an essential part of your journey? In what ways can you continually evaluate and refine your approach to skillful means in order to further support your spiritual growth and the well-being of those around you?

NOTES/REFLECTIONS

IS THIS OVERKILL?

The author examines the concept of "overkill" in relation to spiritual development and addiction recovery in this chapter. He contends that the severity of addiction and the steps required for recovery are frequently overlooked by our society.

The author emphasizes right away that addiction is a disease that permeates every aspect of an individual's life, not just a bad habit or a lack of willpower. According to him, addiction develops a false sense of self and a distorted personality that strives to avoid discomfort and pain at all costs. The true self, which the author refers to as the divine image that is inherently good and yearns for union with God, is concealed by this false self.

According to the author, addiction is an effort to fill the hole left by the absence of one's true self. It is an erroneous quest for wholeness that yields a flimsy and fleeting sense of fulfillment. According to Rohr, a person can only recover after reaching their lowest point and realizing how inadequate their false self is. They can start their spiritual journey toward healing at this point of surrender.

He talks about the Twelve Steps' function in drug and alcohol recovery and emphasizes how effective they are at assisting people in undergoing spiritual change. He emphasizes that the Steps are a flexible framework that let people customize their journey to suit their particular needs rather than a rigid set of guidelines. The Twelve Steps offer a way to reflect on oneself, accept oneself, and surrender to a higher power.

The Twelve Steps are brought up by the author as a potential "overkill" in the fight against addiction. He contends that this criticism results from an ignorance of the severity of addiction and the steps required for recovery. In response, he argues that addiction is a serious and all-encompassing disease that calls for an equally serious cure. According to him, the Twelve Steps are a generous and all-encompassing approach that addresses the mind, body, and spirit of the whole person rather than being excessive.

According to the author, recovering from an addiction involves more than just giving up harmful substances or bad habits. It necessitates a total change in one's identity, as well as a fundamental adjustment to the way one thinks, feels, and interacts with the outside world.
He stresses the importance of thorough introspection, honesty, humility, and a readiness to make amends.

The author also examines how religion plays a part in addiction recovery in this chapter. He acknowledges that organized religion could have drawbacks and occasionally aid in the creation of a false self. But he contends that spirituality, which transcends all boundaries of religion, is crucial to the healing process. He defined spirituality as having a strong bond with one's true self, other people, and the divine.

The author reiterates the importance of a comprehensive strategy for addiction recovery as she closes the chapter. He places a strong emphasis on the necessity of realizing how serious addiction is and the radical self-transformation that is required. He encourages readers to follow the Twelve Steps because he thinks they provide a tried-and-true route to recovery and spiritual development.

In conclusion, this chapter explores the idea of "overkill" in the treatment of addiction. According to the author, addiction is a serious illness that calls for a serious cure. He defends the Twelve Steps as a thorough and forgiving method of dealing with addiction, highlighting the significance of introspection, acceptance of oneself, and a spiritual path to recovery. A holistic understanding of addiction is also demanded, and he exhorts readers to follow a transformative path to recovery.

Key Points

1. In relation to the twelve-step recovery program, this chapter examines the idea of surrender as a key element of spirituality.

2. In this chapter, it is discussed how, contrary to popular belief, true surrender actually requires a great deal of strength and courage.

3. The willingness to acknowledge and accept our helplessness over some aspects of our lives, particularly addiction or harmful behaviors, is regarded as surrender.

4. The twelve-step program places a strong emphasis on surrender as a means of breaking free from the destructive habits that have imprisoned us.

5. According to this chapter, giving up or losing is not the point of surrender; rather, it is about giving up control to our egos and allowing a Higher Power to work on us, resulting in transformation and healing.

EXERCISE TEN

1. Spend some time thinking about the concept of "overkill" in your own life. Consider areas where you may have a tendency to go above and beyond what is required or appropriate. Write down three specific examples of times when you have gone too far in your thoughts, actions, or behaviors. Consider what prompted your reaction and how it may have affected you and others involved. Finally, consider some other, more balanced approaches or responses you could have used.

2. Think about overkill patterns you've observed in your life. These could be recurring themes or behaviors that appear in a variety of situations. Make a list of at least three overkill patterns you've noticed in yourself. Consider the underlying causes of these patterns, such as fears, insecurities, or previous experiences. Consider how these patterns may be impeding your personal growth or causing you or others harm. Finally, consider strategies or actions you can take to break free from these patterns and cultivate healthier, more balanced responses.

3. Practice mindful awareness to become more aware of moments of overkill in your daily life. Choose an activity or situation in which you tend to go overboard, such as cleaning, organizing, or conversations with loved ones. Pay close attention to your thoughts, emoti-

ons, and bodily sensations as you engage in this activity. Take note of any signs of excessive striving, perfectionism, or rage. Take a few deep breaths to return to a state of mindfulness and presence. If you find yourself going overboard, gently remind yourself to take a breather and find a more balanced approach. After the activity, reflect on your experiences, noting any insights or new awareness that arise from practicing mindful awareness in relation to overkill tendencies.

Self Reflection Questions

Have there ever been times when you overreacted, exhibiting excessive control, perfectionism, or unhealthy dependencies?

_____

_____

_____

_____

_____

_____

How has finding balance in your life and letting go of overkill tendencies been facilitated by practicing the spirituality of surrender and acceptance?

_____

_____

_____

_____

_____

What actions can you take to address and heal the areas of your life where you might still be having trouble with overkill behaviors?

_____

_____

_____

_____

_____

How has the act of submitting and accepting humility changed your perception of God or a higher power?

_____

_____

_____

_____

_____

How can you practically apply the concepts of healing, surrender, and acceptance in your daily life moving forward?

_____

_____

_____

_____

_____

NOTES/REFLECTIONS

AN ALTERNATIVE MIND

The author delves deeper into the concept of spirituality and its role in addiction recovery in this chapter.

He begins the chapter by stating that the primary problem with addiction is the dualistic thinking that lies at its heart. Addiction, he explains, is a symptom of a divided mind that seeks to fill a void or numb pain through external substances or behaviors. He contends that the mind is not meant to be divided, but rather integrated, and that true healing and transformation can occur through this integration.

The author then introduces the concept of an alternative mind as a necessary component in the recovery from addiction. According to him, the alternative mind is a state of consciousness that transcends the dualistic thinking of the addicted mind. It is a non-dualistic way of seeing reality that accepts paradox, accepts uncertainty, and acknowledges the interconnectedness of all things. This viewpoint enables people to transcend their limited ego and access greater wisdom and compassion.

The importance of spirituality in cultivating this alternative mind is also emphasized by the author.

He contends that traditional religion frequently perpetuates dualistic thinking by providing simple answers and binary choices.

Spirituality, on the other hand, encourages people to go beyond dogma and engage in a personal and transformative relationship with the divine, whatever that means for them. Individuals can break free from the cycle of addiction by developing a new way of seeing themselves and the world through this spiritual journey.

The author investigates the intersection of spirituality and the 12-step program used in addiction recovery. He observes that, while not explicitly spiritual, the twelve steps can be viewed as a spiritual framework due to their emphasis on humility, surrender, self-examination, amends, and service to others. He then contends that incorporating spirituality into the twelve-step program improves its effectiveness and allows individuals to connect with a higher power that aids in their recovery.

To support his arguments, the author draws on a variety of spiritual traditions and practices throughout the chapter. He discusses Jesus', Buddhism's, and mystic teachings, emphasizing the common thread of non-dualistic thinking and the transformative power of spirituality. He also emphasizes the value of contemplative practices like meditation, prayer, and

and silence in developing the alternative mind.

Finally, this chapter explores the concept of an alternative mind as an important component of addiction recovery. The author contends that dualistic thinking is at the root of addiction and that spirituality is required to cultivate a non-dualistic perspective on reality. He investigates the overlap between spirituality and the 12-step program, emphasizing spirituality's transformative power in breaking free from addiction. The chapter draws on a variety of spiritual traditions and practices, emphasizing the significance of contemplative practices like meditation and prayer. Overall, the author makes a compelling case for the role of spirituality in addiction recovery and offers practical advice on how to cultivate an alternative mind.

Key Points

1. The chapter delves into the concept of "alternative mind," which refers to a new way of perceiving and thinking that is necessary for spiritual growth and transformation.

2. The alternative mind is distinguished by a radical openness to mystery and the ability to hold contradictions, paradoxes, and tensions without requiring immediate resolution.

3. Contemplation and meditation are practices that help people detach from their egoic thinking and connect with a deeper sense of self and the divine.

4. Individuals must be willing to let go of their need to always be right as well as their attachment to rigid beliefs and ideologies in order to cultivate the alternative mind. This enables a more compassionate and inclusive way of thinking that goes beyond dualistic and judgmental thinking.

5. Individuals with an alternative mind can also see the interconnectedness of all things and embrace a worldview that values unity, interdependence, and love. It makes deep transformation and healing possible, particularly in the context of addiction recovery and the twelve-step program.

EXERCISE ELEVEN

1. Spend some time journaling about any new insights or perspectives you gained from the reading. Consider how the concepts of an alternative mind challenge your previous beliefs or understanding of spirituality and the twelve steps. Write about any questions or doubts that arise, as well as any additional research you might conduct to deepen your understanding.

2. Gather a small group of friends or members of a recovery or spiritual community to discuss the chapter. Share your reactions and thoughts on the author's ideas on the alternative mind and how it relates to spirituality and the twelve steps. Encourage everyone to contribute their thoughts and engage in respectful dialogue about the implications of his teachings.

3. In accordance with the concepts discussed in this chapter, set aside some time each day to practice mindfulness. Choose a specific activity, such as eating, walking, or breathing, and focus your attention entirely on the present moment, without judgment. Notice any thoughts or emotions that arise and gently bring your attention back to the present experience. Consider how this practice expands your awareness of the alternative mind and its potential for transforming your spirituality and engagement with the twelve steps. Keep a journal to record your observations and insights as you continue your mindfulness practice.

Self Reflection Questions

How has cultivating an open mind and heart helped you better understand and connect with your higher power?

_____

_____

_____

_____

_____

_____

What are the barriers or obstacles that prevent you from fully embracing the alternative mind?

_____

_____

_____

_____

_____

_____

Have you noticed any patterns of resistance or defensiveness that prevent you from exploring new spiritual paths or ideas?

_____

_____

_____

_____

_____

How have your preconceived notions and judgments hampered your spiritual growth? What can you do to challenge and overcome these biases?

_____

_____

_____

_____

_____

Have you been able to let go of your need for control and certainty in your spiritual journey? If not, how is this preventing you from experiencing true transformation?

_____

_____

_____

_____

_____

How can you cultivate a sense of curiosity and openness in your spiritual practice, allowing new insights and perspectives to challenge and shape your understanding of the divine?

_____

_____

_____

_____

_____

NOTES/REFLECTIONS

WHAT COMES AROUND MUST GO AROUND

The author believes that the idea of karma is a crucial one in the process of healing and spiritual growth, and this chapter goes into more detail about it.

The author starts off by stating that traditional Christianity has frequently overlooked the concept of karma, mainly because of its connection to Eastern religions like Hinduism and Buddhism. He contends, though, that karma is a universal principle that holds true in all facets of life and is not just a concept found in these traditions.

The natural law of cause and effect is represented by karma, in his opinion. It implies that we can have either positive or negative effects from our deeds, thoughts, and intentions. He emphasizes the fact that when we harm ourselves or others through addictive behaviors, we set up bad karmic patterns, particularly in the context of addiction and recovery. Up until we recognize and deal with these patterns, they will keep happening in our lives.

The author uses the teachings of Jesus as an example to demonstrate this point. Jesus stressed repentance, which entails confessing our sins, making amends, and ultimately altering our behavior. He emphasizes this in his teaching. In a fundamental way, this procedure fits with the concept of karma.

The author continues by saying that the metaphor "what goes around, comes around" can help one understand the idea of karma. He claims that the negative energy we release into the world eventually comes back to us, entangling us in a vicious cycle of suffering and compulsive behaviors. We need to engage in the process of soul work, which entails sincere introspection, asking for forgiveness, and making amends for our transgressions, in order to escape this cycle.

In relation to the twelve steps, the author emphasizes the significance of steps eight and nine, which call for compiling a list of those we have wronged and being prepared to make amends. He emphasizes that this step entails more than just expressing regret; rather, it entails making an effort to mend broken bonds and right previous wrongs. By doing this, we not only free ourselves from the bad karma brought on by our past deeds, but we also widen the door to healing and change.

The author also examines the concept of collective karma and makes the argument that our society's problems are a result of our collective actions. He thinks that society's addiction to power and materialism is the cause of many systemic problems, including poverty, inequality, and environmental destruction. He suggests that in order to solve these issues, we all need to accept accountability for our deeds and work to build a more fair and sustainable world.

The concept of karma is explored in depth in this chapter's final section, along with how it relates to the process of healing and spiritual development. It is emphasized by the author that karma is a universal principle that encompasses all facets of life and is not exclusive to Eastern religions. He emphasizes how crucial it is to take responsibility for our actions, seek to make amends, and undo any harm we have caused in the past. So doing allows us to escape unfavorable karmic patterns and unlocks the door to healing and change.

Furthermore, he makes the argument that collective karma is a factor in societal problems, and that it is our collective duty to address them and build a more fair and peaceful world.

Key Points

1. The concept of Karma, or "what comes around must go around," is present in both Eastern and Western spiritual traditions, albeit in different ways.

2. According to the psychological and spiritual concept of Karma, our actions and intentions have consequences, either in this life or in future lives. It is a method of comprehending cause and effect as well as the interconnectedness of all things.

3. Understanding the principle of Karma can help cultivate awareness and responsibility for one's actions in the context of addiction recovery. It can encourage people to think about the consequences of their actions and make decisions that are consistent with their values and higher purpose.

4. Karma also challenges our tendency to blame and blame others, reminding us that we are responsible for our own actions and have the ability to shape our own destiny. It encourages us to take responsibility for our decisions and to seek personal growth and transformation.

5. Finally, the concept of Karma encourages us to live our lives with mindfulness, compassion, and integrity. We can cultivate a more harmonious and fulfilling life by considering the impact of our actions on ourselves and others, and by aligning our behaviors with values of kindness and truth.

EXERCISE TWELVE

1. Take a few moments to consider the phrase "What comes around must go around" in the context of your own life. Reflect on any patterns or cycles you've noticed in your relationships, behaviors, or experiences. Write down three examples of situations or circumstances in which you have seen this principle in action. How has this knowledge changed your perspective or actions in the future?

2. Think about the positive aspects of your life that have come full circle, or instances where "what comes around" has brought blessings or growth. Write down at least three things for which you are grateful that have returned or been reciprocated in some way. Reflect on how expressing gratitude for these experiences can help you cultivate a sense of abundance, trust, and flow in your life.

3. Think about an area of your life where you feel stuck or stagnant. Consider how you might be contributing to this state and how you can use the principle of "what comes around must go around" to effect positive change. Identify one concrete action you can take to break the cycle, such as reaching out to repair a broken relationship, letting go of a destructive habit, or seeking support for personal growth. Write down the action step

and commit to completing it within a specific timeframe. Think about how the potential impact this intentional action could have on your life and the lives of those around you.

Self Reflection Questions

How have your actions and choices contributed to the patterns and cycles in your life?

What recurring themes or situations have you noticed in your life, and how have they affected your spiritual journey?

_____

_____

_____

_____

_____

In what ways have you taken responsibility for your own healing and transformation?

_____

_____

_____

_____

_____

_____

Have you actively sought to break destructive cycles and patterns, and if so, what has been the outcome?

_____

_____

_____

_____

_____

_____

How have you witnessed the positive and negative consequences of your actions unfold in your life?

_____

_____

_____

_____

_____

_____

_____

How has your understanding of spirituality and the twelve steps influenced your ability to recognize and address repetitive behaviors or thought patterns that impede your personal growth?

_____

_____

_____

_____

_____

Are you willing to surrender control and accept the concept of "what goes around must come around," trusting in the greater wisdom and guidance of a higher power?

_____

_____

_____

_____

_____

NOTES/REFLECTIONS

AN UNEXPECTED POSTSCRIPT/ONLY A SUFFERING GOD CAN SAVE

The concept of a suffering God as a means of salvation and transformation is examined in this chapter.

The author begins by recognizing the contradictory nature of Christian belief in a suffering God. He claims that traditional Christian theology has placed too much emphasis on the concept of a perfect and distant God, leading to a misunderstanding of Jesus' suffering on the cross. Recognizing God's suffering, he believes, is essential for spirituality and personal growth.

He then delves into the idea of redemption through sharing in Christ's suffering. He explains that in order to experience true transformation and salvation, people must be willing to enter into their own pain and connect it to humanity's universal pain. Only then will they be able to truly find healing and forgiveness.

Furthermore, the author emphasizes the significance of forgiveness in the healing and salvation process. He suggests that forgiveness is beneficial not only to the person who has caused harm, but also to the person who has been harmed. Individuals can free themselves from the bonds of their own suffering and find inner peace by letting go of the resentment and anger that arise from being hurt.

The author also investigates the concept of solidarity with others' suffering as a means of spiritual growth. He contends that true compassion and empathy can only be developed through an understanding of the world's universal suffering. Individuals can broaden their hearts and deepen their spiritual connection to God by actively engaging with the pain and struggles of others.

Finally, he emphasizes the importance of accepting the paradox of a suffering God. He contends that true salvation and transformation can be found by embracing our own suffering, connecting it to Christ's suffering, and extending compassion to the suffering of others. We can become vessels of God's healing and love by living in solidarity with the suffering world.

The author challenges traditional notions of divinity and salvation in this chapter, urging readers to accept the concept of a suffering God. We can find true spiritual growth and become agents of divine healing by connecting our own suffering with that of Christ and the world, practicing forgiveness and compassion, and living in solidarity with others.

Key Points

1. The idea of a suffering God challenges traditional understandings of God as all-powerful, perfect, and beyond suffering. This chapter explores God's paradoxical nature as a suffering God who enters into the human experience of pain and struggle.

2. The chapter discusses the theological significance of Jesus, who is seen as the ultimate embodiment of a suffering God. It implies that by willingly entering the depths of human suffering, Jesus offers a radical form of salvation that goes beyond mere intellectual belief or religious ritual observance.

3. The chapter explains how the image of a suffering God can alter our perceptions of compassion and empathy. When we recognize that God is intimately present in our suffering, we are called to extend the same compassion and understanding to others who are suffering, rather than judging or blaming them.

4. The author reflects on how the popular phrase "God has a plan" can sometimes perpetuate a harmful theology that justifies or dismisses suffering. Instead, he emphasizes the importance of acknowledging and emb-

racing our own pain as well as the pain of others, as it is only through vulnerability that true transformation and healing can occur.

5. The chapter concludes with an invitation to reflect and meditate on the image of a suffering God, allowing it to challenge and reshape our understanding of spirituality and the path to healing and wholeness. The author contends that by accepting the reality of suffering and recognizing God's presence within it, we can discover a deeper and more authentic spirituality that leads us to a compassionate and loving way of being in the world.

EXERCISE THIRTEEN

1. Spend some time to reflect on the concept of a suffering God. What does God's suffering mean to you? How does this idea challenge or broaden your understanding of God? Write down your thoughts and feelings in a journal, and consider discussing them with a trusted friend or spiritual mentor.

2. Engage in a simple act of compassion for someone who is suffering. It could be a friend, a family member, or even a stranger. Take a moment to listen to their plight, offer a comforting word, or offer practical assistance. Reflect on how this act of compassion strengthened your bond with the suffering person and

how it connects you to the suffering God.

3. In times of personal suffering or despair, intentionally seek out stories or examples of individuals who have found hope and redemption in the midst of their pain. Read a memoir, watch a documentary, or listen to a podcast that tells the stories of people who have endured and overcome adversity. Think about what these stories teach you about the possibility of finding hope in your own adversity. Write a letter to yourself, expressing words of encouragement and hope for the future, grounded in faith in a suffering God who can save.

Self Reflection Questions

In what ways do you personally struggle with the idea of a suffering God? How does this challenge your faith or spiritual understanding?

_____

_____

_____

_____

Think about a time in your life when you were suffering. How did this experience shape or deepen your relationship with God?

Think about the importance of compassion in the concept of a suffering God. How does your understanding of God's suffering affect your capacity for compassion toward others who are in pain?

Reflect on the relationship between suffering and redemption. In the midst of pain and struggle, how does the idea of a suffering God offer hope and healing?

How can the idea of a suffering God inspire and empower you to find meaning in your own and others' suffering? What impact does this understanding of God's presence in suffering have on your perspective on life's challenges and difficulties?

_____

_____

_____

_____

_____

_____

_____

_____

_____

_____

_____

NOTES/REFLECTIONS

FINAL EVALUATION QUESTIONS

How has reading the book influenced your understanding of spirituality?

_____

_____

_____

Were you able to connect with the author's perspective on integrating spirituality and the twelve steps? Why or why not?

_____

_____

_____

Has reading this book changed your perspective on addiction and recovery? If so, how so?

_____

_____

_____

Were there any specific passages or concepts in the book that spoke to you? How did they affect your self-awareness or approach to recovery?

_____

_____

_____

_____

_____

Did reading this book provide you with any practical insights or tools that you intend to use in your own recovery journey? If so, what were they?

_____

_____

_____

_____

_____

NOTES/REFLECTIONS

NOTES/REFLECTIONS

Made in United States
Troutdale, OR
11/28/2023